OTHER WORDS FOR GRACE

ALSO BY MARGARET CHRISTAKOS

Not Egypt

OTHER WORDS FOR GRACE

Margaret Christakos

THE MERCURY PRESS

The publisher gratefully acknowledges the financial assistance of the Canada Council and the Ontario Arts Council, as well as that of the Government of Ontario through the Ontario Publishing Centre.

Edited by Beverley Daurio
Cover design by Bryan Gee
Author photograph by Scott Mitchell
Composition and page design by TASK

Printed and bound in Canada by Metropole Litho
Printed on acid-free paper
First Edition
1 2 3 4 5 98 97 96 95 94

Canadian Cataloguing in Publication Data

Christakos, Margaret, 1962-
    Other words for grace
Poems.
ISBN 1-55128-017-5
I. Title
PS8555.H675C8 1994   C811'.54   C94-932108-7
PR9199.3.C4708 1994

Represented in Canada by the Literary Press Group
Distributed by General Distribution Services

The Mercury Press
137 Birmingham Street
Stratford, Ontario
Canada   N5A 2T1

ACKNOWLEDGEMENTS

My appreciation to editors of the following journals for publishing selected poems from this manuscript: *line, West Coast Line, Fireweed, Prism International, Poetry Canada Review, CV2, the League of Canadian Poets Living Archives*; & to the Writer's Reserve Program and the Works-in-Progress Program through the Literature Office of the Ontario Arts Council, the City of Toronto through the Toronto Arts Council, and my mother for extremely helpful financial assistance.

I would like to thank: bpNichol for what he keeps teaching me; Joanna Gertler and Lynne Fernie for flexible jobs when I needed them; Nancy Chater, Betsy Warland, Victoria Freeman and Pinelope Gramatikopoulos for provocative readings and creative kinship; Lee Ogden; Joy Tataryn; Jenny Rose and Claire for glimpses back into girlhood; Beverley Daurio; Bryan Gee for the beautiful cover; and all the friends and family who surround me like an alphabet. *Especially B & Z.*

Memory is a marvellous derring-do of fiction-making and truth-telling. Grace revels in the juggle.

This book is dedicated to 381.
"Words" is especially for MaryJane.

Text that appears underlined and in italics is from *Not Egypt* (Coach House Press, 1989).

CONTENTS

Forewords   9

DECIPHERS

missing/harsher sentences   13
Palm Reading   21
Hollywood Squares   24
Lacunae   25

THE GRACE PAPERS

Lateral Burn   31
Insinuations   37
Hangman   47
Target Practice   48
Special Effect   51
Cure   53
Influence   55
Wise Cracks I: Not Olga   61
Graze   62
double & tender   64
Home Economics   67
Groom   69
Superstar   70
Flushing   72
Uppity (a spiritual)   74
Words   76
Wise Cracks II: Jawbreaker   81
Saying Grace   83
Wanton   85

SOOTH

Serum   89
Case Work   92
Bridge   94

Forewords

1. What are the connections that shape the proximity between our power as individual women to speak—which can mean to be received—and our collective power to redefine an order of reality that remembers all of the differences among us? This is a question on a lateral field of feminist consciousness. Think of this field as an enormous spread of cells. All of the cells are your own. They belong to you and speak with your remembering. They have your little-girl face. She is good, that is to say I would essentialize this, her goodness; and like any single cell she lives by an intense motive to survive. By both of these truths, she is Grace.

2. i remember nothing of my girlhood until i begin to remember the accidents. My broken toe on the right foot gives me back 1973. A thin layer of cloudy skin lifting off my young chest burnt by the steam and boiling coffee: 1972. And just as if a noose had slipped around it, my bare neck singed by a boy's kite string, a torn memory of 1966. For eight years solid, my back teeth repeatedly catching on a ridge of scar tissue building itself on the inside of my cheek, then the metallic rush of blood onto the tongue, & me jumping up from the dinner table running to the mirror and howling OW OW OW OW. What were the excess words stored up and kept in the flesh inside the mouth? What inversion of power left me only the "ow" part, the hurt cicatrix, the words eating themselves back into pure muffle? Don't know, can't say, hard to tell. But soon the cells speak, saying *it was no accident*, for as Nicole Brossard has often reiterated, "To write: I am a woman is heavy with consequences."[1]

3. My house was built into a rockbed, into a circumference of houses ringing the crest of a high meandering hill. It was never the city centre though, because my house fronted on a circling cul-de-sac which existed on the orbit of a mining past, and standing on my yellowish lawn, between the maple and the spruce, I could see diametrically out over the sulphurous layers of slag-heap horizon to the gleaming shaft of the INCO Superstack. The vertical order of all things in a town like this had proceeded from the gouged-out rock, up along the insides of this monolithic exhaust pipe into, well, *oblivion*. Oblivion, in this case, was sixty miles away in North Bay, according to a model of progress premised upon a city that would tear the guts out of its

own middle to proliferate, and forget what went missing as quickly as possible. I wonder, where does the rage go when a single cell is scooped inside-out? Where does the memory of disassemblage go when its pieces are shipped into clouds festering one-way east or north to rain on the taken-for-granted soil of another middle? But the Sudbury women had agreed their children should breathe this new cleaner, fresher air, not attending to the hidden part, the fallout of a concentric consensus built on belief in our centrality. Is it this lacuna that opens my eyes? That it is just as often women who invisibly conduct each other into the order, both through our intense wishfulness for a mother/daughter similitude, and our seeming non-correspondence to more villified hierarchies, like the multinational president ordering his Department of Progress to build him a Stack like none other. For it is women who have taught me to "hold my tongue," how to hold my mouth closed but always partially open, lodging deep ambivalence in the scar tissue. The double-bind of the female poet has often been to bring all of the body but none of the cells, none of their troublesome memory that tends to startle smooth orations of concentricity. I want to write about an enormous spread of gossiping cells. All the cells are also my own, are my body's, as they are the city's I grew up in. They speak with a future power of remembering *more, hard to recall/ what gets lost in the memory of/ erased is always/ more*. They have an old-woman face. She is wise, that is to say I would essentialize this, her knowing; and like any simple cell she lives by an intense knowledge that there are no accidents. By these truths, she is dis-graced, which is to bring all of the cells along with other words for Grace.

1. See, for example, Nicole Brossard's *These Our Mothers, Or: The Disintegrating Chapter*, trans. Barbara Godard (Toronto: Coach House Press, 1983), p. 45.

DECIPHERS

missing/

Searching back for the moment
intersection of wind on the face
that gives reality its blistering effect
mark on memory
placement of the comma
separating past from remembered present
the moment it happens

so often the wind

footfall

running by dozens of
collaged colour shape fragrance
shop windows in concept but in the running
just blurs of motion moving backwards
rewinding the tape machine
contiguity of ambiguity
of reverse momentum toward
what

on the face what brushed it
how the light performed contact
if it was hot or cold

if there was contact
how it felt on the face then
as if now

About the poetic line
how it keeps reticulating
carriage snapping back
revising entry point
zigzagging back in syntax

car on automatic pilot
veering in fits & starts to
the last chance hotel

You pull me with you
my hand caught in your grip
moving suddenly left   right
backwards to a new beginning
let's take it from the top
this grip jags
motion of the whole body
coerced

& so in the writing
i canter forward falling behind
collapsing in the wave of telling
to a past story
capitulating to the brainy grip of memory
digressing to the rear
carriage return
spasms of

not that i don't want to go

Getting used to this narrative
disruptured in a dozen places & what else
like moodiness on fast forward
papers shuffled, piled up & fanned apart
the nameless card is desired
name of never, this time
not the one, still seeking
like the rustle of pilot
over short grass
low hum of the search
for the missing woman's body, girl body
premised on her missingness
always, this seeking

cresting through weed banks
swamp
actual grave sites
parting long strands of treed vision
moving through in a forward motion
combing hillsides, parks
every possible detour
scavenged
for her body, missing several days now

the smiling head with sparkling eyes arti-factual

Women missing their
our
bodies
sending out memory posses
search parties, peering
under residential porches   sheds   summer garages

all the nothing places

measures taken

Not sure that i ever wanted to go there
where the grip insisted
how the body moved into that space
leaving the smiling head behind on a photograph

taken aback

young girl's body gone missing
maybe in all the nothing spaces
tricky spots read as blanks most days

space of the alley gutter path alongside the rubble
terrible with possibility

where her body might be without the head
or sparkling eyes

How to keep insisting
i return to
crux of
how common it is
the beginning, moving backwards always
to where the tape gets significant
shuffling
reticulating
insistent repetitions of scrabbling
backwards

wanting the moment of blisters
wind on the grip
what coerced the moment
to intersection
inserted breathing space;   memory

Where the wind goes through the smiling head
into the missing body
suffusion of
syntactical contiguity the line wanting to spin
out from its centre to evoke colours shapes fragrance breath
lightly exuding
what she loved to look at in the particular shop window
that stopped her footfall quick on sidewalk
what she wanted to be happening
her breath on the vision of her choosing
reflected back to her
where the eye wants to return to
the space she wants to look into
be inside of
find her own body there

the line about where she finds her own body sleeping beauty
leans to kiss it
her
our

missing bodies

/harsher sentences

Why parts of her seem missing   (body, memory)
but also
colour shape fragrance accent

skin.

On the table now: what abhors it
how our white supremacist eye defines value
if it is good or black

if there was value
how she carried its markers
outside & then in

Questions hang in the middle like a car mirror
ever present
awaiting my glance
framing me

i realize i'm always in the centre
in the middle of the car
in the middle of the highway
in the centre of the city

my city   (in the daytime)

in the middle of a mobile day, the questions glance back
with harsher sentences

If she had been
a black girl
native girl

asian girl
latina
would her smiling six-year-old face
grace
the flashy front page of the *Sun?*

this is a hardest question, one of the hard ones.
would it?

Whose deaths do we let go by
not noticing who the we is
not bothering to make official
a fuss of
her absence

these terrible ellipses;
how to grieve over the bodies of the dead girls
with these questions
knotted in our middle

how to bring all of our bodies back into the present
knowing without her to begin with
most of our stories wouldn't even exist

the dead girl instantiates the male detective hero
the twin peaks of his epiphanies, his profanities
his plot

a grave plot

twisted plot
twisted mind

the blond-haired blue-eyed boy next door
composite of the scarborough rapist

what a plot twist, fingers

pointing right back to centre

•

When tricked into joining the obituaries
the subversive woman finds herself
challenged to resurrect all of the links
between massacre
& mass occurrence

to plot twists in old logic
insurrections of memory

to let none of us go missing without a fuss
without all of us remembering *more*
hard to recall   what gets lost in the memory of
erased   is always
more

Each woman's skin colour shape breath accent
lightly exuding
what each differently loves to look at
in the particular shop window
each different face reflected back to her
as *good*, as *memorable*
that stopped her footfall amid syncopated rhythms
what the rhythm means to her
what each of us might want to be happening

the space where each of us
finds her own body
differently
via the mouth   archaeology
delivered to this moment

Palm Reading

1st   hand filled with kiwi skin
furry & solid nugget
enclosure of a small hand

girl was smallish overall probably younger probably young

noticed surprises
that she was small & therefore young & that the arm
stretched its full length along the torso
& at the bottom that the hand was cupped

child body in fetal position & the right hand
curled around solid soft fruitish possibly kiwi—
was warm, wasn't it?
yes

had soft furry skin?
yes—
girl-woman's brain leaps—
not apparent
take my word, not a

•

2nd   cut into frame:

the whole older male body leaning back in its chair
evening ambience full with
cultural norm, *of course*
a flickering television

male in frontal recline a refutation a non sequitur

adult body on scale with the remembering mind
what?
not child body with outstretched arm
& shocked/
shocking
handful

•

3rd   child gaze, deep irises open-lidded
deflating balloon
red sac de-gassing?
de-gassing
without perspective of bodies
contact
no
because subtracted from view

we will see where this leads, mind you

•

4th   trying to book a room
in a bed & breakfast where she's stayed before
keeps insisting the room exists
& would/should take her in, why not?
don't ask me

trying to book room back into her own body
well
this much
& being turned away at the front desk

"yes, such a room exists

but it's preoccupied...
sorry..."

so the line suggests &
the hand doesn't dream
but

•

5th   dream-people with AIDS
calling up for reservations
in their own past
favourite rooms

& the woman says
"fine, come to my house"
all the "rejects" coming to her house
all sleep in the beds of her siblings

the way it happened, certainly

what about the kiwi?

hand still appalled & burnt by recognition
her dark continent, christ

little red balloon hissing out air
losing consciousness

a kiwi is not compared   unless

the hand doesn't lie, either.
I've plenty of experience
in these matters

Hollywood Squares

Shaped by the Father's fiction. The patriarch whose face cuts a Hollywood cleft in the handpainted softness of her dear father's silverprint image. Chisel and gauge. Tuck her girlhood's lack of guile into this cleft. But she nestles near his mouth, yearning for the relaxation of his lips into her <u>perfection</u>. Her small arms and legs in a white sleeper blossom from his teeth like an orchid. Film-noir cigarette smoke. Or the way your mouth opens onto a swollen tip. The 1920s backdrop of immigrant ships crossing to America with seeds fingered nervously in pockets like particles of a new language. Why can't she breathe Daddy into this cleft? And her mother's self-ordained presidency of the Canadian Sinatra fan club, her unmasked passion, then. A time-lapsed exposé of the classic female fan mirroring the emotional pitch of her idol. Streaming tears into the architecture of both their profiles, Sinatra's and his, her father's. Then, it is for her drinking this preposterous man into the sexual throat, a buff-glass bottle of Coca Cola. Brown liquid eyes of a child-boy and through their lens to daughter's guilt at mistaking her parent for Sinatra, Clift, and the patriarch equally. Who's in her chin? she said, seeing her father glimpsing from a dim angle inherited from the stylistic biases of continental court-painting. From each darker slit a pointing hand withdraws. You too can see yourself in frame. Shaped by the image's falseness. Her father's particular clefted chin looks on, like she would, eyeing the cloaked photographer. Wanting to achieve a "little man" illusion—for his longish curls are coded differently now, undercut by his buttoned white collar. The flash stipples her guilelessness. She poses, ready to adore the chin he holds just above her shiny black bangs. She wants to kiss him relentlessly. To blight his distance. Make an imprecation on his star quality, where she can see herself talking, the sound turned low, her miniature lips below his father-kiss. *Frankie,* you say, *do it now.*

Lacunae

A bucket, solving archival, nattering worries about overflow, exchanges her self-wrought consciousness (as if she too is beside herself) as rent for the room's foremost corner. My body is ten feet away, moored on cushions for sleeping. The distance between us is analogous to the ultrasonic image of a small cyst positioned three centimetres to the lower right of my left ovary. Or something, too, like the relationship of Prince Edward Island (sanguine, ragged, afloat) to mainland eastern Canada, though here proportionate sizes are exaggerated so as to disqualify the image.

The roof water enters and erupts my resting. I accept the image, the roof water ruptures inside my pelvic carriage, and discounted histories of islands gone missing are, it seems clear, recuperated. A land mass waves fimbriated announcements (silent) to whatever tiny egg might end up encoding its mother tongue. Found again the way language inside a finger or penis begins to feel like water, placed at a distance in a smooth glass casing, or earth, the husk of seizure, loss, & grasping.

Who charted these waters, anyway? The baton measuring abnormalities in my cradled pelvis swirls in gel, draws out the cyst's territory, my hip proffered for access. I am three centimetres from accepting this relation; the PEI sand dunes are fallopian in memory, fringed with thirst, not to mention myself, ten feet from the bucket (engulfed, radar-poor) reassembling the distance from one woman's fertility to her daughter's. Besides me, who cares that islands sink like a whole language into recess? Or that even benign relations create echogrammatic mappings of my experience, then abscess and sink again, speechless, into sites of discovery? My daughter to be named "laguna," the uncharted (pool, pit, gap).

THE GRACE PAPERS

Lateral Burn

the carpet soaked with milk

Each lens, each turn in the view   a part of speech
dropped exegesis.

scene 1:
Hollows lush with plant growth, green
sprouting from a blank slate   Grace
walks through her speech on stilts   avoiding
references to regional landmarks.

Grace whispers (hisses)
"this bitch goddess molds me with rubber gloves."

take 2:
My mother and I look nothing alike. Her arms are much longer
than mine, but our difference according to scale, as thesis,
lags. Transmission of dream matter, in my eyes where I carry it
from the first photographs   utterly birthwritten.
My mother and I are mere mirror images   mère
in another language neither of us speaks.

Women often find this seductive, that the mother rebirths herself
in daughter flesh. Our potential to conflate histories
as if we did not write this sequence, this time/space narrative
    of sloughing off or away from. We inculcate simultaneity.

[Anger, hostility, outbursts
all inappropriate
for Grace. Let's get this straight   from the start/
from the hoarsest mouth   (oops!)]

profile
Lips merge   congruence, the pink
brown resilient entreaty
the inter-view
of lips pleasuring each   within   inner

concentration.

So you see the glass fell to the floor with a smash
unprecipitated: my body made also of breakable junctures
along which you may decide to turn.
                              If you followed suit
the crystalline structure of tuna in a can might (add water)
reconstitute fish-in-sea veracity. Shatter
the Production of Order
Domestic. Resisting.

•

Where in her body are·   memory, its   plurality
I assume of arms and legs like mine
a conscription.

Looking sideways, I guard the slower motion
of my repositioning as a younger female, but
past childhood,
framed in the threshold where kitchen became Hall.
The white-painted walls columnar, me
central in my enactment.
Central inside my comptrolling agency
I was an agent of servicing family
familiar; my body

and in this role, congenial.

Let my hands lie palm-flat on the white surfaces
which compare me to a fiat.

The moment skin laps on paint
marking its fleshiness in contrast,
then I replace it above.
Many-armed body servicing me at the centre.
Again   a threshold, what is important
& the smallish body
in its relationship of humanness to House,
to acts of will, maybe.

My fingers pinioned around the mug handle.
Steam provokes me (a stage light)
incites my slow muscle to lengthen
allowing for the neck's pivot sideways.

Father stands behind me   near the stove
hot liquid still percolates
emanating bean urgency
"fresh coffee"   a signal in the air.   My service

makes me credible, young person
with boundless impressibility   could
be folded with airplane wings to
arrive upstairs fleet of foot

body of cardstock, then, or
a practice of plastic.

•

The young hand carrying adult "brew"
after dinner. Doctrine of ingratiating
myself to Good, oh to be thought of
well. The coffee contract.

Tendon, for a second, twitching   unsure   as my eyes
measure the distance from my thumb
warm now by association with ceramic...
from my thumb's nail, half moon sunk
in the bitten-off crescent

                                  this distance
measured precociously
to his eyes.

We exchange contact. Intercept each other's
acceptance, the doldrums of these rituals
Why can't mom get her own coffee
Why do I enjoy this duty so, what do I mean
enjoy.

•

In the neck there is a certain code.

At a trigger/angle such as this
neck speaks an aperture of parallel knowing
third eye.

•

Six or seven feet, in metric about two metres.
My thumb   heated   to your trim capable chest,
& your one hip crooked to support your arm.
You seem well-suited to the post-dinner
solitude and frenzy of the kitchen
breathing in coffee utopia
as it is performed   encore
the illusion of laissez-faire.

My hand right where it should be at the given time
I am "cooperative" and "competent"
small girl with a job older than myself
tithed, the body. In a harness I might dramatize
if it weren't for sub-walls of whiteness
propping me in relation to memory
the starkness is what gives it back to me
this doorway.

At the kitchen's exit I get dizzy with transition.
Panicked at the hearth's loss   as if tearing   & then
thrilled to be in the uncharted hall
orphaned   unsexed   pre-pubescent   without gravity
or able to suspend disbelief in
the family order   dissolving

reprise:
In the anarchic, almost, hallway
where my toes encroach   this
attraction.

•

On the level of skin, this is about burning;
the hot liquid in the mug carried by the serviceable fist
He's got the whole world   in His Hand
becoming transposed.   Inverting the world
a cup of coffee   chalice of duty
so her chest is a scarred map of
renovation, where the heat moves to
with consequence.
Knowing what the hall meant, & how to draw
them all to the middle, reverse
ascensio.

Stripped then   of the shirt
lifting crosswoven threads out of the "skin"
clear sailing to the hospital
Grace emblazoned & wordless
tracking her "dark continent"

Insinuations

Climbing.
Grace is shrinking her legs
into the stout peggish ones
perfect for rock climbing, evinced by the boys' example.
She has her runners on,
a plan to run.   Agenda

to scale the rocks
lift up one half of her body
hoist it like a kite   concentrate of
    burying oxygen in the lungs' lowest reserve, pumps
hydraulic will
to yank up the other
half

There.
She's climbing. Acclimatized to height, to gauge
whose territory this is, whose map she's impinging
on, the brink of discovering
over there, whose fort.   Theirs.

Timmy's. John, Neil, Thomas
all bigger, the boys.

The huge-seeming hill, & what it brings on as she clambers
discombobulated by the pure
wind.   So sharp!, forces a shift

in Breathing,
                    her breaths of air bigger than below,
have to be,   billows &
puffy thrusts of its coolness
infatuate blood, haze her vision
a special
effect

to be transported, like, later on, in
Star Trek, excitement
at the level of each aggressive cell, all shaken up
left gasping for consciousness,   oh
the wonder of science...

Neat! What it's like to be here, this high on the hill
silhouetted in frame with the boys
who intensify,
as Grace sees them in the foreground, prematurely
pop through the slit of what she's yet
to imbibe, to be let in on

where she glimpses their secret society
holding court as in *Lord of the Flies*
another core text for later
she's pre-viewing
    entering the primal margin of the "rocks"
just as if it were their island, rehearsal space   re:
her   sallying blithely, or curious
into this land, this plot. Unprecedented.
The first grace period she's allowed.

•

She's an explorer from the outside.
Unmistakeably. Their deliberate black sweaters, bomber
jackets & matching toques
precede her, mark how cold & little
she is on the hill, self-conscious
about her earnest red slicker,
beloved three-tone beret & coordinated mittens, and Scarf
furled stylishly for street-level panache
flowing back over one shoulder

which now forms a pulley for the *mean* wind
tugging at both of the fringed ends
its agency seeming to turn on her, to double
up & tighten   conducting itself differently
on this terrain.

Why the hell is her scarf so long?

   like a leash, a flag.

a way to coordinate little girls
on street-level, & outside of this, suggest
the risk of strangulation. Wrappings of meaning.

•

Have I really written what this hill means to her?
How she loves the craggy rocks
like her own hands, feels skin
when at night the horizon she projects
is that range, ragged black edge incising
uncharted planets, mysterious
beyond the rooftops.

& above, striated glow of the sunset or sunrise
kissing the body of the rocks' outline

that she thought what kissing meant
was perfectly that line

light and rock

where her eyes take it in
seam of her lips unspoken

ciphered instead by the rocks

& wishing
& the vision

the kiss she wants to climb into

oh, *Wuthering Heights*, yes
Wellington Heights,
Sudbury,
Ontario.

Utopic.

Can't be topped, though, mounted by the girl
but she wants it
Wants.

•

Later, how the southern Ontario snobs
defame this miners' town, its moony slag-scape
rotten press of coal heaps
bleak bastion of redneck ugliness
their *shittiness!* about this Beauty
which is her body too,
that horizon

•

First there's the circle of road & sidewalk
cul de sac they live on
that belongs to all the kids. A carnival, most nights,
with caravans of two-wheeled bikes circling for hours
into driveways, over manhole ruptures, soaring
halfway down the street, then backtracking,

a parade up & around, endless. And in the middle of the circle
rotational games of four-square, skiprope
the chants & bickering of their juvenile court
carved out of every evening, somehow
they could organize all this *and* sequences of twenty-one
beneath the basketball hoop enshrined by Mr H
on the city telephone pole at the circle's head.
Inclusive,
or she will remember it this way
having been included.

Then, the parental ring of houses
& somewhere inside, all the mothers & fathers
puttering through early evening, loosing the grip
of mutual surveillance,
the children's of them, & theirs of the children

                                        Summer evenings

& the easy permission everyone had
for oblivion. Concentric
consensus
            to stay relevant to the dominant geometry
reproduction of the circular order
cunning
pre-structured
with conspiring effects,
no wonder they didn't need the adults.

•

So it's clearer
why Grace would desire the canyon, out back
where the boys ritually disappeared
& she could track their prodigy
only by kites which taunted of their prodigy
they boasted.
How they boasted, those ciphers

in the distance,
zone of the flying boys, little lords
way past the circle's boundary
& her, not
invited, not at all, not assumed.

Such a long scarf for a little neck.

Around the neck there is a certain code,
drawn on by the precedents
& tight.

She's climbed there though, & now
Grace leaps to the line of actual boys
in one impulse strips off the scarf
so her bare throat, its pink skin, scintillates with chill
& nervy imaginings, something like Cathy's throat licked
by desire on the moors, its bareness
flagrant, a new flag
jigged up the mast of each kite string,
implied.

Configurations of this dimension, like vibrations of a belly-laugh
too subtle, outstrip their line-up altogether.
Become a bird's-eye view
of the stringent house window
way across the street she can peer over at,
imagine the phantasm of her small face straining
   & then this laugh
   of the naked neck coming through her
   of light and rock
& her ex-centric afternoon.

She's never felt such a brazen wind.

She's never felt brazen, like a boy, before.

●

& they sense this, sense her possibility
and the need for a ruling now
a Code.

> *she's too little to have a kite, don't*
> *give her a kite, let's not*
> *let her*

The letter of the law,
who the us is, how quickly this is
cleared up, ruled & lorded over the rocks' body.

> *yes,* the boys say, *let's decide this.* & do.

Grace hasn't much then, but to read
the comic-book cast levitating for the boys
at the tips of their taut, wind-stroked strings
crests of the DC Superhero kites
flapping in whizzy obedience
against a technicolour blue sky.

As if the boys would fly in kind
if they could fly
it would be like the blue and black capespans
of Superman & Batman
remotely in their likenesses, unleashed
like the high stakes
up for grabs between Man & Space
the classic frontier where no man can really go

where the kites are sent to penetrate
the boys would penetrate
that ampersand.

Grace gets whoozy watching the swooping flight-path

of each kite, perched in air   how they pitch & glide
striping the sky,   how they lock it in multiple, vertical,   hold.

She can't think now what a kiss would mean.

Can't think a horizontal kiss,
the rock split from light,
colonized.

She thinks maybe she got here too late.

•

What happens next is a metaphor
for Grace's nerve
                    (of steel? of stealing?)
how she's dared, like an extension of the boys
to climb onto this turf
to insinuate her naked neck
into their midst, to say
like a flag-pole from another language
hoisting its unreadable cipher
that she wants
Wants this
I want this too, she is suggesting.

Of course, Superheroes have Superpowers,
why the boys use them in their own place
to do such flying! & so it's Batman
keenly paranoid
who pinpoints the alien among them

            threat to the new empire
            let's radio the Superlord

wires singing, zing   buzz   click
manifesto high in the sky

zeroing in on its target
radar of a bat
very handy here.

In his sights, in ours, since it is us too
sighting her,
                    to recapitulate:
Grace is 3 feet, 2 inches tall.
She has a red slicker, striped
hat & matching mitts, and a band of bareness
between the light, or her *vision*
and the rock, or her *body*

By desire & design, she's risking her neck
in the space where a kiss belongs
according to her legend
of how the moor is her room topsy-turvy

& how she's climbed outside,
with consequence.

•

If this were a video game, it would look thus:
the knife-edged string of the Batman kite
on a reconnaissance mission for the new empire
acts to attack, & singes a skin-deep burn
    like an edit, a solution
across the undeniable target of her neck.

You see, logically, a burn
to terminate the naked threat.

This is known as the Decapitation Warning Move.
As a rule, to insinuate off with your head
is highly effective.

The empire rarely needs to go further,
& therefore speaks of itself as Civilized.

This is the second grace period she's allowed.

The space she's left with, where the neck
might begin
& might stop, simply underscored

a red emphasis, deft stroke of the vertical
inscribing primacy over her horizon
What the moors *can be*, anyway, when you're too close
to see them...

The special
effect
of distance, which blurs
proper perspective, imbibed
i.e., what the other girls might desire
once Grace's passion is delivered back to centre
like an accident

•

Questions for the classroom:
    a) What did Grace imagine the rocks to be?
    b) Do you suppose Grace was a popular girl?
    c) Could you suggest how Grace might have worn her scarf
       so its length was more manageable?
    d) Name your favourite Superhero.
    e) List, if you can, five colonies of the British Commonwealth.
    f) What do you think this poem reveals about the author?

Hangman

Of all the words Grace pronounces
Of all the riddles she messes up in memory
Of all the nerve she's mustered
Of all the

directly behind the bridge of the nose
sewn into the hollow between brains

For the love of her fort-building club co-members
For the love of Him on high and His red-nosed reindeer
For the love of Mrs Lindsey's *grade six grammar-tongue with a Georgian drawl*
For the love of

If only she hadn't peeked
If she only could've been patient for five minutes, breathing evenly
If she could only know
what's good for

the relationship is a triangular web

In the first place you have to guess
In the second place you better think hard
In the third place don't expect me to help   cuz
it's up to you, girl
why don't you take the chance,   love
is all around Grace
is all around
alphabetic & easy as
 a b c why don't you
ache / bake / fake / make / quake / rake / take / wake
it it it
time's up up & away

Target Practice

When tricked into joining the military
the subversive woman finds herself
hovering near ammo bunkers   & at night, dreams of
a tin shack ticking   incipient grenade caps
itching between front teeth
delivered to this moment
via the mouth   ontology
of a real target practice declared
from her underhanded position
out from under   & the careful aim
     she's taking

It really is about killing, then,
stabbing in the back, face
about face   really is blood in the bull's eye,
language cut open. All these "commonsense" acts go
through the sieve of the throat,
retch, clear-sighted
Bitch coughed up,
expressed as in detonated,
let loose

Would you just *listen* to what's
coming out of your *mouth*, young lady, you/   gap of
Despicable

Unspeakable Young Woman,
waging offensives.

•

When tricked into joining the military
Grace slips her ankles inside chaps
marrying herself to stilts again

The minefield looks like a city promenade
big city scintillating "tits" everywhere in silk
Grace's own newer chest in a fashionable
halter dress, rainbow-coloured
target of whistles, hoots
inspection she passes swimmingly

Mom can't quite believe the ruckus,
raises eyebrows at Grace
then at The Men, at the brink of an outburst inevitably
returns to Grace; concludes
that dress is too revealing dear
the hotel's close let's go   change

But but but   but but   but

•

Sites of ambush she records later:

1. Stairwell of the museum, no one else around
attendant too close   chesire smiles she's
the most "beeyooteeful"   does she realize her rank
among women?   he crowds in, eyes glistening   Grace
evades   quick feet hitting marble stairs tap tap tap
like teeth, dropping out of her smile
him receding *phheww*   air whistling through her empty mouth
evacuation orders transmitted and received
manoeuvre complete

2. Open panorama of the park, a deep pit from surface mining
camouflaged with short grass   now public leisure space
Grace strides by,   wind in her skirt where she admits
she wants it;   & then their clucks   distortion of birds
into fallout   shards of shark talk crazy men

grinning or crooning or eating   their gums on her shoulders
chewing skin like tobacco   swallowing
pieces of women's bodies   her body
then spitting it out like it tastes bad   or the taste's
all used up   expedient & spat back up   traces on sidewalk
the sound of *ex pec to ra ting*   what did she expect
dressed like that, her mom's voice in that crossfire   dismembered

Hard to recall yet more, but there is always   <u>more</u>
she forgets   gets lost in the memory of   erased

3. But at least the one about the waiter, umpteenth
tuxed serviceman   uniformed   pompous in his section,
boss on leave on a cruise ship near the Greek Isles
steering clear of dirty linen, all that crap & crêpe batter mix etc. etc.
     So these boys   boyish to Grace who notes
their steamy eyebrow lines & trembling curls   youthful
hunk-y, she'd tell Tanya & Lorie about these ones   *only in Toronto*
they'd sigh
     These men spot her as she enters the split second it takes
to name her body competent and cooperative *thank God* she incants
her body terse & moving   tracked by their *um hmm*s & *oh yes*es
how she knows she's in situ
on the front line   her mom "somewhere"
                                        for cover,
mama's neutral arms where Grace loses
later, her young halter   unhooks it & the stripes from her skin
& crawls between cool hotel sheets   loving this woman supremely
     glad for her steadiness, & tireless forgiveness
     how she offers it & advice, makes Grace   wonder
how to love them all without casualties, her mom   those men
the dress   the city   this day suddenly blurry, weary,
& falls to sleep clutching her stilts for good measure

Special Effect

It buries its face in Grace's soft, warm neck
holding itself in the space of a kiss
where it doesn't belong, then pulls back
& says you are loved

now at a distance
it undresses, undoes the pants
& oversweater, slips out of, off it
but as it leans forward
below shirttail is the cock
long vertical excess
pointing straight down like a rope
the body floats above

& Grace's eyes fill up with its excessiveness
in that space, with those words

where the tongue is sent to penetrate
it would penetrate

Then it adjusts the whole body
notices how its tongue is outside itself
how it's swollen at the head
puffy with how outside it is
& tries to push it back
inside the underwear slit: ampersand
men can remain dressed behind
while the tongue exposes itself
a band of bareness
high stake between Man & Space
erected in the frontier
of her *body*
crosscut by
her *vision*

full with consequence
with language,   full
patertongue

Cure

Waiting face down on the couch
Grace imagines sleeping, leaving,
slipping through an intercom
into Starsky's thighs, enterprise *come in*
or meeting the real Charlie,
a voice-mail visionary
even then

Her chest whoops & throttles hard protest
against pale blue blossoms
upholstery like a mother's dress
or the stuffing it held, soft prop at least
of a plump female torso, her absence
undermining, couche-
mère
where the doctor was instead

Syringe poised above Grace's naked cheek
requisite nightie hiked to the waist
her calves skitterish
as a colt's
she was supposed to know to breathe casually, recite
how now red pin
so-fa to go, Mrs Robinson
glide into good health
as the needle bursts
unburies
lights a cigarette

But the case studies she's blueprinted
from Nancy Drew, Cherry Ames and the Angels
pique her sixth sense, a strange vibe
rolling eyes in the back of her head
due south to investigate, the nose
sniffing along for good measure

Three secret agents
using her spine like a fire pole
without a blink or missed breath
landing footsure & soundless at the sacrum
at the scene of the needle's crime-
wave about to rush in
   like greased light
           n
           i
           n
           g

& then her thunderous Jump, Jolt
of muscle & skirmish, counter-
whooping the needle's prick
up up and out of there
bucking it out of her field

her feeling

Paralyzed then. Numb to the navel. Grace's mouth
speaks like a smoking gun into pillow
while around her, floodlights switch on.
Cut cries the doctor. Canned laughter
is called in to understudy

as Grace, no wing-wearing Angel,
is hitched to a Charley horse, tendons swollen &
reined in to the plot of an ordinary sitcom, Godiva deposed
& rebuffed, for weeks after, the pink double-sting
of losing her cool and her saddle
propped like a lost badge on the
chesterfield

Influence

Between the inside & outside of
sleep
Grace fakes a passage
bartering memory   chocolate   chiaroscuro...

Modigliani's models were aberrantly tall, she decides
& always *leaning*   through *his* eyes

Small mouth roving like a moon from the outside
past the baroque mirror attendant on vampires
scanning the fisted piano & egotistical sofa
all in grisaille except for, repeating, a mouth like a moon
& home-movie murals of shadows of leaves
lucent, flickering on walls of the living room

allegiances, how they grow in her

Of van Gogh's sunflowers what she appreciates
is arrogant sourness
curling back her top lip she calligraphs
"flow-er pow-er"
 into the night silence

    & judges the art prints tainted by their attitude
under the so much more beloved
mirage of leaves from the maple

insomnia
                a meandering
                                        fuse

like op-art on a black page
inside & outside de facto
indeterminate
pre-determined

•

When she first opened the Peter Max poster catalogue
it was to participate in her mother's gaze
or to be seen

to research a birth certificate at 3 a.m.
probe into the coffee-table museum
its neatstack of source material
for her mother's sunday morning enchantments
    each book winning fascinated grins
        independent moodiness
a private measure
coded between the coffee mug, a slow cigarette
& her mother's lips   absorbed
in outside
dreaming

The generation gap, thought Grace
not comprehending contemporaneity
until she entered her own *yellow submarine*
topsy-turvy turf of
fantasia, finally

a clue to her mother's threshold for the
cutting edge where
inside & outside became
interchangeable, & her mother less puzzling-
ly modern

Still Grace's desire—
    narratively trained for stories leading to sleep,
        not dreams,

& still wishing this
betting even chocolate for it—
Grace's taste for certainty & tradition
grows tentacles
against the fridge-drone of difference

•

A poster is not memory
but something outside
turned inward

   like Max's looping cable-y free-
falling equation of
women's mini-skirted stances   (twiggy-hips
jutting)   draped in chiffon &
paisley psychedelia   hands becoming hillsides,
roots, branches   & curled-back eyelashes
convoluting toward butterfly abandon with
daisies everywhere   (Grace's namesake flora)
intoxicating surfaces of sidewalk & bellbottomed pantsuit alike
female chameleons becoming each other & the background
or what used to recede
now animate & aspiring to selfhood

pizzazz, what might have attracted the mother
emancipation of women's contentment
from dictates of form, &*energy*

libidinal lines erasing
more than they traced

•

Night moves between Grace's mouth & the page
like proto-polyester waves riding each model calf
belonging to the myriad
of tall tall women's elegant calves
essential as Grace's whole nine-year-old torso

surreal women striding with stilt-sleekness, mandating
make a splash!   knock 'em out!
lip-synched with duplicitous savvy
through buff orange kisses
words balanced over & under
the space the lips make
red-hot as six-inch virginia slims

Grace's apprenticeship in ambiguity
how to balance the female mouth
    never quite opening it
    never quite closing it
co-ol &
hot, double pleasure of the smooth one

inside & outside sleepwalking on a love train
like memory from any·opening, smoke genie
whistling beyond the maze
of compartments & platforms, high wheeze brandished like
a ticket to ride

away

•

The mother's almost-stylish apricot-coloured lips before work
branding Grace's cheek inside
the mother
outside

as close as she can get after a point
detesting the sweet wax cosmetic smell that sticks with her
the taste of the smell

drawing on her mother's mouth
so modern,
a metaphor instead of mama's mutter
imparting an era of new storylines
where the ending disguises itself on purpose
operating on motifs   repetitions
a gesture: the mother's mouth,   touching

•

Grace's own mouth imagines speaking, & closing instead, mute
framing, perhaps resentment   or willingness

proliferated by dim outlines of the art prints

She feels what she remembers of living room decor
for comfort like the back of her own head
filling in what's indelibly shadowed
concrete memory of the mother's imagined gazing
time/space catalogue for the wee hours
Modigliani
she's always loved that name
holding it just above her clenched mouth's roof
transspatial attic of sensation
turning it slowly over
in the deep red palette
of leaning women's necklines

& their curious but unflinching birdlike noses & sleepless eyes
topped with off-kilter pillbox hats

pinned into place
against the less decideable background
sombreness

they too sit in pitch black rooms
one per page

Wise Cracks I: Not Olga

Granted:

> *one across the big toe*
>
> *one between left / right*
>
> *one where the head detaches*
>
> *one twinning her vision*
>
> *one the stitches disguise as a bat*
>
> *one where thighs cleave to the buttocks*
>
> *three where the teeth wouldn't come*
>
> *one of pink lace, collaring the continent*

but by non-olympic standards, a perfect
ten

(none of the pure body, her unbelievable vaults
and the new chest like a bentwood chair back)

At summer games, Grace's best score was always *midi*
below the belt, further, the knee

along the blue vein, toe-bound
to falter &

O the limp she had

* Olga Korbut, Russian gymnast, gold medalist in the women's floor exercises competition at the
1972 Olympic Games.

Graze

Blades on frozen lake elide her anxieties
about rarely seen friends, relatives, she'd rather
skate until dinner bells
thrash frost's amphi/
theatrical silence

As soon as winter's miracle
of breath   bright outside herself, puffy & close
comforts enough for december
                         january
                             february
Grace recuperates her high skates to whiteness—
   vinegar to lift salt from the boot tops
   soft shammy to encourage tongues out of hiding
   runners ground to a glint
   new laces keenly yanked—

& each saturday, stakes her balance on one blade's front teeth
a ballast dug into ice, seeking the stroke that's launched
a thousand hips, then *finds* it, & pitches through in a forward motion
removing snow from her path like a long scarf, flamboyant
strip/   tease of the sole
like Magnusson gone to the ice capades

   stroke glide stroke
   thighs pump to inner tracks *this is not*
   a "Puppy Love" this is
   a snow job uncovered, bliss
   of surpassing her
   missing self etched
   then lost again

well, after gold what's left but
scissor strokes to the rear: perfectly good lines crossed over
                                 whited out, her odd jour-

knee
    tucked & chin up, Grace chases her fingers to the tip of nightfall
as if her future grazes at the rink's underside
a dervish magnet pulling from beneath
that keeps her figuring past herself
& the present's unmarked finish line

At least in this routine
she loves these circles of scintillant privacy, gravity
she gives herself leave of,
                leaps over

       (wordlessness,
       that double axel)

                      & glides back to
one beginning or another

* Karen Magnusson, Canadian, Ladies' World Figure Skating Champion, 1973.

double & tender

Not noose, she is saying
nous. French for you & me together.
It's all Greek to him though
his olympian lips empty
like they will never be again when he is older
will never speak this innocence
Grace easily fills up
with her eleventh year's excess
of parallel knowing, her
third eye.

1. There's a cola bottle lodged in the small desk's ink well.
2. Both of his gauze-wrapped ankles fidget over the faded carpet.
3. They love to play school, like this, on the weekends.

•

When her brother leapt from the garage roof
to the driveway's frozen thud thirteen feet down
betting Batman, Superman
the earth moved a little
ruled exceptional amnesty
to receive him feet-first, a
double entendre

But in the anarchic, almost, stairwell
where her eyes encroach   this
family attraction for adventure
takes heart again

& Grace's cooperative spirit,
sticky from heated soupbowls she carries

from incandescent kitchen to the TV room below, this *spirit*
follows her contract of cracker crumbs back to the landing
where she finds herself again, absentminded & usual, *fine thank you*,
stalled in the starting blocks of her stilts;

not much to do   but survey
the space she's left with
from the base of the stairs   eight feet of
      tallness   zigzagging up & up to the flat
         hallway & threshold   of vegetable-strewn
            dinnertime   to the bright main course of
                              kitchen again

Paused in the foyer
Grace overhears a duplicit
promise of ascensio
six o'clock TV news story she traded the soup for:
      a woman's voice unstrained through a megaphone
      bitching mighty & clear over the airport P.A.
      leading the Air Traffic Controller Union strikers
      against another unliveable wage freeze
how she unspeaks with a nerve of steel
corporate double-
talk, its circular order
of silencing,
                  & Grace imbibes this,
breathes these angry-angry-real-lady-words into synch with a motive
(i.e., *not seeing her kids in the early evening so she dreams them invincible*
onto a plane motioning at my fort in the canyon
& then a dozen planes start exploding, bursting into mortar,
& she cries NO but the planes break overhead anyways, & her kids & the metal
crash down as if it's some kinda target practice
& I'm sleeping in the fort, sleeping
beauty but the twist is, her kids aren't mortal!, they're SUPERteens
who swoop down like kites to save me but in the Nick of time from the
Grip *of fate, hey, just like*)

her brother.

Well, in a chaos of choosing
like this heroine's job at radar central,
Grace sniffs up the staircase, catches wind
of the far-off top step
the what-if of going
where no girl goes lightly

& *leaps,* then, to imagination
(leaving her name in the margin)
strips the dishtowel from her bare neck
& pushes off to arc over the full height of stairs
    one giant step for girlhood

FLYING is what she wants
the flight up from under to *over*
to fl̲y̲
          —like her little brother's miracle
          a floating nun without the damn veil
          a transfuse memory—
insurrecting the time / space narrative
of Lois Lane riding vicariously on Superman's coattail
as if she too enjoys her soup-serving coffee-serving dream-serving
du̲t̲y̲ so,
what we could mean *to enjoy*
if our buoyant cells
like ciphers from another language
sailed over the body
of the rocks' outline,
for once & ever *dis-*
    graced &
        full

Home Economics

That Saturday afternoon
what Grace tries to teach him   is
there's nothing accidental
about the Cruel Leg-Hold Trap,
nothing unintended when the jaws snap
or how it's buried underfoot just waiting.

His first assignment is to draw a picture of it opening
& closing, almost open &
then closed, to put a leg
right in it, in close-up.

Grace defines *unaccidental:*
the way the staircase scissored open
stretched from tall to intolerant
for tenderizing effect,
how it was she ended up
with a foot in her mouth, appeared
to trip herself & toe the line with *des* feet
her biggest toe on the right foot
(obviously the wrong leg to be pulling)
knuckled under five times
& brought down to earth
with consequence

Punctuated by five needles then
set inside
a parenthesis of crutches
her gamble bracketed back
into the vertical
        order
of landlocked *wishing*
                    & *the vision*
both tithed & familial, yes
unaccidental

it was her body;
not his

The fruit being
not sour grapes but
what she has to show him—
a dumbo thumb, a bandaged pogo—
her brother's doubled-back luck
la chance in any official language
swaddled inside the pillow Grace loads her toe onto,
like exhibit A: of having known
exhibit B: of having wanted

What each gets
from among the standard elements
depending on who the control group is
how mortal is defined *et bien sûr*
the proper execution of
variables

Then he lists for ten minutes the names of the food groups
plans three properly balanced meals (no more than two veg. per meal).
The last thing is the word
she dares him to guess in Hangman
which is from another language
neither of them knows yet, *radar*
spelled backwards.

Groom

Grace is visited by her great-gram while reading a Harlequin
& studying Rousseau

Gram whispers: *you're the spitting image*
                 of my woman image

                 hair, mouth, certain attendances
                 a servile definition
                 role made entirely of contingent lapses
                 correspondences
                 shaping round indentations in a beach
                 since this has been done before
                 subscription to historical forms

Leaps into a nude beach
fields of unripe cotton
a she-bear
cunted human
what skin, what a soft organ for pleasure
the pores repeat breathing

                 when I was a girl

Groom encroaches, groom tabulates.

The sheets buckle from so much "groom."

Grace wakes, her mouth reciting
HER LEAN BIRDING HANDS MARRIED TO ME PAST GENERATIONS
OF HETEROSEXUAL PURCHASE

a transfuse memory

Superstar

Alone in a room, Grace always lip-synchs
popular songs by women radio stars
whose voices closely resemble
her own high   clear   croon

& whose dark hair lends mystery,
worldliness
to her competent, naturally,
duplicitous knack for staying in key
keyed up   under lock &   or is it hook, line
Singer   when I grow up!   /she's a torch
& a little girl, stereo-
typical.

No index here to the anxious playlist's
structuration, though, no striking note pre-empting
"Killing Me Softly" in Grace's tune of femininity
with Yvonne Elliman asking Jesus
"Could We Start Again?" To please. Both fit

the twelve-year-old girl who looks back bleedingly

at two scenes: Jesus & the guy slung with a guitar.
Each strips the ruins of her earnestness
clean of earnestness, to what's left,
her labia   lips uttering
pure letters at the entrance
to feminized sensibility. A love of singing, devotion
    all bloody & bleeding

this strumming of stroboscopic memory
against her face
woah   oh
Grace's mouth & what it pronounced so tunefully:

rapture: flushed, as in fever
rupture: her whole life, in *his* words
long before Grace bled or knew its rhythm

so the words are
Singe-ing. S-injuring. S-inking. Sinning. Signing
his words into her labia
cunting her silenced
    siren,
inaudible

Should not be
the playlist
how it's stacked against her long before she bleeds.
What is this blood, Grace asks,
lost in the inscrutable-to-her plot of *Jesus Christ Superstar*
which goes around non-stop in circles
unturned tables she can't figure,
her lips swollen against that tune
goes round & round & round

teeth tearing into a memory of the next verse
versus this one which she has down
pat. So excellent, Grace's soft recital alone

when the crowd can't hear the words
kill her, the empty room

Flushing

we must forge rock from porcelain, forget our
intensities

The blood won't go down   vanish
as she'd hoped
Grace pleads with the porcelain to cooperate
be operative with her in the feminine project
of disappearing traces   the body makes   *pleeez*
when female

as if to re-emerge menstrual
into L.'s thirteenth birthday party
a Friday Night Evening party with Beer
and Alcool and leather-jacketed jocks
cursed every girl equally. As if Grace
would spill the guts of a global anatomy
sealed up with crossstitches   privatized
ceremonial, seen just once
at a certain time & place which cohered:
     the men briefed in advance
     incense well-distributed to offset the smells
     mothers stony-eyed   rigid   amnesiac

All of them having seen it once, just south of some border
like Flushing, *boy, what a dump/*   a real no man's land
this seeing   in terms of constriction
a passage   attention to: *take a good look now*
a tension;

& in this, a world-view   opened kaleidoscopically
exactly like a cunt in the flow of it
the blood scooping astroturf, the Eaton Centre,
invention of the microchip, liposuction,
multicultural policy at the city council level,

arboreta, the ozone layer
pre-empted by women

breathing a word instead of silence
red tonguey word
whorish seepage
bloody dumping
how incredibly indulgent.

Grace sweats in the tiny room
boys pounding on wood   *gotta piss*   *c'mon*
her heart engorged too with the red cargo
panic   terror   intense shame
all the emotions that make the blood move
why female means hot & cursed, she groans *I*
hate this hate this hate this

Uppity (a spiritual)

Where the stilts lift and
separate Grace's daily planning
depends on points of departure
she requires

For example,
their amazing promise of relief the
breathy
dizziness of relieving
promises she's
offered too smilingly to
solicitous enemies, lighthearted
'n' light-
headed her feet invite buckles
to tighten, squeezin' the streetlife in her
out out and skyward
(a magic attitude made possible
by generous adverts for poise
on command:
get UP!   on the dance floor, everybody)
warded to the fore by cinderella's birdies—
     chirping stepsisters of blind faith and charity
     & the godmother rising above it all, eagle-eyed,
     firmlipped

These backups tug tight the stirrups
adjust the pitch &
her readiness
to rise
until the scaffold of Her Nakedness
uncreases:

ankles/
knees/
hips/
dotted waistline/
busted bust/   GROUND
neckline   higher
(all the scores   to a
she can just hold   itself
together   excusing
not quite open   abruptly
not quite closed)   staircase
a body unfolded upward   wooden
                like a plain

Words

being disciplinary in writing meaning sticking
to the consciously structured
fear of going into unknown territory
"freefall" derogatory (derogated)

A long gash   gut-deep & then scourging toward fresh oxygen
how she opens her mother's lips & closes them

she is the scourge of the gash dis-closing her mama's insides   the deep guts
of her mother are what she moves out of, betrays   bringing along this
opening

for those moments another head with a different brain is the concentric
consensus   around which her mother's widened lips, her speech &
meanings, accede

she takes the words out of her mother's mouth her mouth displaced from
language   language disembowelled of words, her mother's   which she
holds in the gash & involucrum of her wanting   wanting to open
her own lips & close them, graceless,
on gasps of oxygen,
no word then for the displaced mother's

reverberating hollerstretched caw   cussing
cornucopia laugh aloud   collapse,
her scourge of

•

By the same effect of never having seen the bodies of
mother sister grandmother
come these inhibitions against writing anything down

•

Grace's fingertips   translucent as any toddler's
probe inviolate folds of labia
each fold the width of a finger
flattened & plump like a lip & so these are named
her "lips"   (very ladylike)

she stuffs her fingers in under around over the folds   opens them
& closes them, never boring   finds a church steeple, & people inside
introduces one to the other & gets them to shake hands
each hand a finger in width like a lip & so they are surnamed
"lips":   Miss & Miss Lip, specialists in social discretion
tireless companions for Grace's rainy evenings bathtimes
TV commercial ho hums & humdrum of car trips
the two debutante mademoiselles enlist Grace's pleasure
rubbing shoulders, grazing eyelashes, entertaining
each other's fancy,
for Grace, reciting colours
                    the alphabet
                    numbers up to thirty
                    a few words of french
starting with bonjour   "bonjour!"
replies Miss Lip the second, labia to labia
forming a roundness

like the lullaby her mother's melodic intonations
open each bedtime   her voice rolling at Grace's cheek
softly crushing back again toward
the horizon of her autonomy,
by all means receding

•

Across the orange-&-brown hooked rug *past* Grace's runners uncrusting mud
bits onto chilly linoleum *through* the doorframe's partial closure *past* the
sparse but effective family photo arcade with relatives grinning *alongside* the
always-on nightlamp illuminating laundry pile's slightly sour smell of
everyone's underwear & towels & rain-socks in brazen commingling *over*
thumbprinted bannister & draughty window ledge & *down* the dim stairwell
echo of her voice
good night ladies   good night ladies   good night ladies
i'm going to leave you now
alone Grace, with Miss & Miss Lip
tripling her mother's distance   & their freedom
free-for-all
freefall

•

Resurgence of
lips merge   congruence, the pink
brown resilient entreaty
the inter-view
of lips pleasuring each   within   inner

imbrication

of daughter narrative of wanting
the mother's language   what it will say to her
lips it might open (opened)
& close (closed)

de-speakable (sic)
between them

birthwritten by this system

•

From *Home Birth in Seven Easy Steps*

1. I am holding my mouth open so that my teeth don't rattle against each other

2. I am holding my mouth open holding what my mouth has on hold

3. I am mouthing a space without closure

4. In every mother/daughter narrative there are two interpretations, a mouth within a mouth, each holding the other partially open & also closed

5. I am condoning a space between my lips to suggest openness so that we might speak if you also have this desire for partial closure only

6. This metaphor is a way of holding mouths partially open & also closed to keep utterance on hold away from rattling since the rattle in our voices would shake me & I am trying to hold on

7. If the opening dis-closes you to me my openness in relation to both our partial closures might open & we could begin to get somewhere

•

Textbook cases, daughter pulling through the mother's mirror image gut-deep in commonsense & wordlessness

•

Grace's love
for those moments
her own head's will to utter
opened & closed
her mother's lips this
transfusion confusion suffusion fusion
too gashing
for words between

a privacy
like fresh oxygen
in the lungs where she carries it, meaning

how they look so much alike, later
but always through a language neither invented
the mother lip-sunk
by daughter flesh   (literary convention of sloughing off
      or away from)

Transmission in breathing then

the abhorred body / absorbed body / absolved
in loving   concentric loathing

always loving again

always loving again

moving back to
these words *mama & me*
to inculcate simultaneity

Wise Cracks II: Jawbreaker

oust (sss

At thirty all three wisdom teeth speak
in one tongue, make their senses unpack the OW
hollering from inside to be yanked out

As they come, the two on top
gossip like debutantes of her teens and twenties
two decades stored above the boneline
solid calcium nuggets smooth as earrings
ready to be held on the outside,
like songs

The third is semi-
perfect, Grace's ten years of girlhood
stuck on their sides, stubborn with their love of horizons
how first she saw things sideways
then in halves

This rectangle of glare—
like a look from her eyes, lost gleam
tendered in the lower left jaw, a clue
hidden beneath small talk and foodstuffs—
grew, not two, but three long roots, & knowingly
dug down for the count of thirty

So the excavation is not a pretty thing:
but a crack shoot, the knife
sectioning and digging
bringing forth the hard matter line by line
fragments of the white-hot look of her
on the inside

this sparkle she's most needed & strategically stashed
like other basics hidden between her head, her
heart,
            throwaways in the throat
not humpty dumpty or hunky dory
but hints of a square name
held undertongue like a lozenge
hunkering at the end of each swallow
getting lost in the marrow,
for good

Angled as language
through the rusty head of a needle,
now it nudges cracks in her smile
snapping the spines
of a hundred chameleons, *not egypt*
but elliptical, like the gum-pink giveaways of as many
sunny bikini-clad ads for vacations to the coast, the hostess
with the most testimonial to
pretense
when it was always there
            the chalky rock soon to crack up on shore, & scatter
            boxy bullet, bitesize and bitter
            cubic tidbit of knowing otherwise

How the wisdoms revisit in small packages, as they're able,
good things the size of baby teeth, tip-offs
of the present listening in on the past
seaming the pieces to wholeness
for a gradual story of origins, evidently
Grace's *ragings*;
the tooth's fear

Saying Grace

once the three molars
are wrenched from their pockets

once the fourth's absence is adequately excused

once her toe stops pulsing
like a heart's lost relative

once she stops shaving the soft pits, long
calves

once the North American map on her chest
holds the breastfruits up to good light

once her laugh is no longer bisected by rope

once her blood waves goodbye with a smile

once upon a time when she is skating

once her palm dreams of itself glowingly

once her garage is neat, tidy

once the island reappears on radar

once her bet on coffee and chocolates is won

once her crutches root and grow roses

once she swims upstream
without leeches or watersnakes
slipping out of her ankles

once she stops reading obituaries

once his penis stops bruising

once she stops grinning at mirrors

once she becomes what she wants

once the crowd hears her recite the word _____ .

once she is no longer craving

once she sleepwalks in daisies

once her body is a mother all around her

once she keeps breathing

once she breathes words of it

she will have herself to thank

Wanton

I am 3 feet, 2 inches tall
running over the rockiness of the past's outline
into her eyes and

scaling that imperfect line

between open, enclosed

&

independent

Ma me embrace, ampersand
of words lost
in the grip of
silences

what they have said to me
how I look back on them, wanting
my senses to touch me
touch to make sense
not the con or the trick
just to sense her there again,
       concentrate of

rocking *in her body*
alight *in her vision*

how I climb inside,
am deciphered
without consequence

SOOTH

Serum

Grace's cunt is throbbing. Though not with this language, or any language she is allowed to hear. But a voice outside the dream carries the words for it, enveloping her body, marking it. The throbbing is language forging its way into her. Not *penetrating*. Sliding, the way wind is swallowed. Always some resistance as the other is incorporated, like cold cold milk, becoming blood. Ooooh. And, oh. Then, aaaaaaah.

She's on a massive ship sailing intercontinentally. Right now none of the continents is in sight. Lots of other boats crowd the horizon. Her arms are thin and long, small and tense. They bend to propel her body along the deck. She's tearing around with this pulsing labia, looking for her lost family and a private room for the cunt which she can't get rid of. It's dogging her, so to speak. Mewing. Miaowing. Rhythmic & inside, steep like under the ocean. Or when one ear is blocked by an aching mucous screen, and the pulse of her brain's lobe, the veins in it, or just her thinking, reverberates like someone stomping down a flight of metal stairs all the way to hell. It annoys her; then again, it's her body, it can throb if it wants to. She is opening to this rare element.

She slows up her crisscross jogging over the slatted wooden floor and starts wondering. Did anyone else's mother pour warm oil into their ear-achey ear? Right down into her head it felt like. The warm finger of liquid being swallowed into who knows where. I'll dream of french fries, mom! Just hold still, dear. And promises it will feel better very soon. How throbbing can be made to vacate the premises, by drowning. Grace makes it sound vile, why? When the memory passes like a soft syringe through her ear, clear to the middle of her vision for that second. Her mom's tender grip on the warmed spoon held in close-up for Grace's inspection. Okay. I'm ready. & resolves her head on the pillow.

The word slides into her ear. Kind of terse at either side but lovely and plush in the center: c un t. Like a long thin arm it sails through the inner drum, down along her spine, though she feels it more in her tummy for a moment, and then the swell of its opening fingers travels like nerve incarnate to her plump lips. The ship pulls into port. The sudden stagnancy of its huge bulk shakes her. Clouds bunch up into a paper bag, set to wrestling, and come inside-out the other side, her brain! It's land, varmints! her dad jokes. Here we are! Grace scrambles down with her sister and they go dashing toward the nearest building.

Just listen to that throbbing! She asks her sister if she feels it too, mouths this through the brainwave radio station they set up eons ago, just for them. Feel the beat, yeah, feel the heat.... She fumbles to touch herself, like a nurse, since this is still public space. She flattens her broadened palm over the apple-shaped mound as if it's her doll's forehead. She's double-checking her temperature. Hurry! she shouts. Hurry, hurry!

Instead of sea-monkeys, a cathedral quick-grows in front of them. Sprouts up and brushes sky. Grace cranes her neck back. As she goes under the gigantic portal she is alone. You know how the sanctum throbs in a frequency that clashes against the individual body? Her pulse is crested out of synch, as though a hurricane passes through her hometown and rips the window frames from all the houses. Afterwards the neighbours roam around picking up lids of garbage cans. Who could foresee such an order to open up on the horizon? And Grace's house, convulsed along the middle seam, one unforgettable cough. The documentary of before and after, and no one stops to ask permission. A moving marker on a constant slide-rule which is, conceivably, happiness.

The word persists, drifting like flotsam at her ear, crashing against the drum like a hoard of drunken teenagers stumbling down a stadium fire escape. Though it is nosing inward, beseeching her, still most people tell her it belongs nowhere in her body, not her mouth, nothing. But the beat wracks her, leaps up and down her spine until it is absurd, a squirrel with the property deed to branches the last tenant sprayed with pesticide, the sticky kind that kills by bondage. What can she do, but leap alongside the throbbing?

For her it is as though the apple Eve raised to her lips was alive with the movement of language, and Eve was ready to imbibe at least a mouthful of its throbbing.

But she doesn't know from Eve, really. The pews of the church are strangely symmetrical and humming, it feels, telegraphing this woman's appetite like some kind of metaphor of her own body. Grace just knows her mother, her sister, herself, and how long and disorienting the boat ride was, halfway round her dream. When she wakes up her mouth tingles as if she's been talking aloud, the lips navigating independently how far off and silken the ocean's horizon is from the scintillant publicity of her cunt, pulsing, which has roused her. My ear's all better! she remarks. Smart cure! Like drinking wind on a milky day so the air and liquid slide in together, into her future, where she wants 'em.

Case Work

Women touching outside the city limits.
Women citing each other, limited by "touch."
Women limited. City-touching. Inside, trying to get out of it.

Grace writes:

I think about my history with tribadism. Being bad-ism! In a threesome? No, alone, just alone; & making connections to wanting to be the active lover, fucking another. Makes me flash to how complex, sad, and weirdly cooperative I've been with many men, egging them in, "loving" to be fucked, & the reverse [*Grace begins to redden*] I'm so prudish! Deathly afraid of being found out, of being invaded here. Old fears. No privacy ever in that house. Always shame about my horniness, which I hid in my back pocket, then rubbed against the bed corner, could get up up and away in a minute. Pushing in circles, digging into the corner, flicking my clit against the soft but specific seam of the mattress under its covers. Earliest memories of lying on the beachball on the front lawn. The inflated roundness taut and companionable under my pelvis. Rolling in a circular motion, hips stirring right out there on the grass! coming. Very young, 4 or 5. Being told to stop. Not stopping, having felt the virtual treasure in the muscles, clenching to tease themselves into peaking. Others peeking, peering, drawing obvious conclusions.

This must be when I discovered the bed corner. Indoor alternative to solve both the public & the pubic problems. This also the era of new growths, antennae sprouting up in every pore, tendrils to keep the house covered. A tender expertise for knowing exactly what happens to a stair when it's stepped on. I became the stair *case*. While the rest of my body did the bed corner thing. Learning to breathe without breathing, oxygen buried in the rush and controlled tremors held low in the lungs, close to the chest, giving nothing away; and still in it, the trouble of near asphyxia and the circling hips below, pushing, thrusting against the bed, taking the weight of my legs, all focused on the spiral grind of bunched nerve endings in the budding come-hither clit Bursting, exuding in the thigh cushions *shhh   shhh* rippling out tight dissipating waves. & as soon as the throb sweet bunching came unbunched like a silent sweettart candy in the wet mouth I was ready again, refurbished. 8 or 9, on up.

Not telling male lovers about this private most pleasurable and surefire technique. The men, who I wanted to hold away from, to keep a space. Or worried they would take it away, work it into "our" lovemaking.

But knowing it was other.

Then feeling her leg & grinding against it & wanting to discover the mechanics of how to make of her pelvis a bed corner & make love to her this way so I felt the come in me & then her on me, before our mouths opened onto the bud itself, or after, mixing the media up and around, encircling ourselves.

And my intense fear of spilling gracelessness onto this page.

No man to dignify the pleasure by sanctioning the act as only ever public, colonized, a holster his hips mean to carry.

Our bodies usually left flat and far from bunching.

"Mmmm mmmm mmm you make me feel sooo good—"

Fraudulence, & the wished-for privacy of knowing another way, bed corner, soft yet posed, the correct meeting of flesh and cloth, layers of it to muffle the edge, protect the clit, measure the body & breath. Counter-balanced layers of fantasy against taboo, wanting it against incipient punishment, rings of sensation bursting like wildflower scents directly into the bloodstream against suffocation, pure muffle. Threat of. Excitement & the closet. Grace's knowing cooped up, lusting, writing something about it.

Bridge

Shift in structure erases my dreaming self. Grace sits on a bus while I inscribe every frame with subtitles. But sitting to write my mind storms my desire, seeking a higher authority re: the assignation of beauty. What's beautiful here? What's the raw material I'll use to achieve the dazzling end-products needed to hand over for approval? And then be kissed. To be kissed! And who sits in my mental cupboard now? Barthes perhaps. Rustling like a nosy mother-in-law. Father-in-law? Oh god. Rustling as a god would in the picking of a sublime apple. "Do you know the consequences?" This is now a Booming voice. Blooming as all voices do once (I) hear them into something raw and welcome. Barthes talks about a love-object. I scan the room like an empress after my newest love. All the rest are pat, owned, but the one that has escaped my tongue—the cheaply dressed servant with her shoulder agape—Gracie, I adore you! And then into this polemic I pour my middle-class consumerism, choosing her forlorn availability. But, maddeningly, this woman does not respond, staring as she is over the gorge of an urban river seeking her own raw material. She is dreaming a moving bus and the desirousness of her search. Abhorring structure but looking for a slave. Her arms are bent and cantilevered at the point where her hands press against her neck; this, really, this is what caught my breath to begin with. What spoke my "access." Now. She has stood dreamy-eyed long enough. "Look for a plot," I snap, <u>stop your meaningless dreaming</u>: there is no productivity without the rise to primacy of an organizing principle. Piffle. Pogwash. I know beneath this. Know I want her, want to own her, to call her mine by my own constructed desire which excludes hers. Want to fawn endlessly over the stretch of her arms bent that way. I lust her subject. She spins at me and says, "Go away, I'm waiting for my lover." My bus lurches to a stop. I get off and walk to the lookout. The cascading river struggles against bulwarks of factory drainage pipes. For the first time I'm interested in fairy tales. The woman below, sitting with her feet dangling in the polluted water, cries tears the size of apples. She lifts her chin and moans, "Mother, mother." When her eyes open I see her. I recognize she is Grace, my great-granny. Like all the women in my family, age has shrunk her body to unbelievably childlike proportions. I fling myself toward her, feeling the bridge spring back from my feet. She lifts to meet me. Our collision transforms us both into teenaged waitresses, wearing gold and red striped aprons and perfectly timing our strides so our opposite arms, bent to carry our trays, are instituted like the symmetry of a sentence. We love We. My face breaks into smiles of uncontrollable joy. The drive-in customers honk, "Break it up." We are wanted in opposite directions. The way refugee families get torn piecemeal from South to North. One country deigns to accept one, the central fringe character, according to its immigration laws. In accordance with the organizing principles supported by the International Council of Desirousness. "We want the one with her arms bent back." But this time Grace is waiting for me. She is dreaming me back into her bus. When I arrive, out of breath and apologizing for my lateness, we unfold our arms and begin to embrace. *What did you dream,* we ask.

ABOUT THE AUTHOR

Margaret Christakos's first book of poetic prose, *Not Egypt*, was published by Coach House Press in 1989, and her poems have appeared in literary journals across Canada, including *Poetry Canada* and *Prism*. Her critical essays have been published in *Tessera*, *Room of One's Own*, *West Coast Line*, and *Open Letter*. She was active with the feminist collective Women & Words in Montreal, and has served on the editorial boards of *FUSE Magazine*, *Fireweed*, and *Women's Education des femmes*. Christakos works as a freelance editor and production coordinator, and teaches creative writing at the Ontario College of Art. Based in Toronto, she was born in Sudbury, Ontario.